GREGORY L. VOGT

MERCURY

Gateway Solar System
The Millbrook Press
Brookfield, Connecticut

Published by The Millbrook Press
2 Old New Milford Road
Brookfield, Connecticut 06804

Copyright © 1994 by The Millbrook Press
All rights reserved
Printed in the United States of America
5 4 3 2 1

Library of Congress Cataloging-in-Publication Data
Vogt, Gregory.
Mercury / by Gregory L. Vogt.
p.   cm. — (Gateway solar system)
Includes bibliographical references and index.
Summary: Presents information on Mercury, the planet closest
to the sun, as it was photographed by the U.S. spacecraft,
Mariner 10. Includes a glossary and "Mercury Quick Facts."
ISBN 1-56294-390-1 (lib. bdg.)
1. Mercury (Planet)—Juvenile literature.   2. Project Mariner—
Juvenile literature.   [1. Mercury (Planet).   2. Project Mariner.]
I. Title.   II. Series: Vogt, Gregory.   Gateway solar system.
QB611.V64   1994
523.4′1—dc20   93-11218   CIP   AC

·Photographs and illustrations courtesy of: National Aeronautics
and Space Administration: cover, pp. 8, 10, 11, 19, 22, 26;
painting by William K. Hartmann: p. 4; © Ron Miller: pp. 12,
15, 24; Jet Propulsion Laboratory: pp. 17, 21.

Solar system diagram by Anne Canevari Green

MERCURY

Wm K Hartmann
Jul 1980

Faster than the fastest rocket, the planet Mercury flashes through the *inner solar system*. The inner solar system is the space between Earth and the sun. It is a lonely region with only two planets, Mercury and Venus. There are no moons, and only an occasional *comet* or *asteroid* passing through.

At an average distance of 36 million miles (58 million kilometers), Mercury is the closest planet to the sun. Because it is so close, it is also the fastest moving of the planets. Mercury whizzes around the sun at an average speed of over 107,000 miles (173,000 kilometers) per hour. That's about ten times faster than distant Pluto moves as it travels in its *orbit* around the sun. Mercury is faster than any other planet because the sun's *gravity* (a force that causes objects to attract each other) is stronger the closer you are to it. To stay in orbit and not fall into the sun, Mercury has to move very fast. Its speed balances the sun's gravity.

◀ The sun casts a halo around a large rock in this artist's painting of what Mercury's surface must look like. The two bright "stars" in the upper right are Earth and Venus.

Because of its closeness to the sun, Mercury has a smaller orbit to travel than any other planet. With its speed and small orbit, Mercury travels completely around the sun every 88 Earth days.

Ancient Planet

Mercury is a difficult planet to see from Earth. It is so close to the sun that the sun's light usually obscures it. The only times to view Mercury are just before sunrise or just after sunset, when the sun is below Earth's horizon and its glare is blocked. Mercury has a dark surface, so only about one tenth of the sunlight that falls on it is bounced back into space. That means that, compared with other planets, such as Venus, Mercury is very dim. Its dimness, combined with the sun's twilight glare and a hazy Earth atmosphere, makes Mercury a real challenge to spot. In ancient times, however, the air was not as polluted as it is now and Mercury was much easier to see. Mercury was known to many people, including the Egyptians, Greeks, and Babylonians.

After the invention of the telescope in the early 1600s, many *astronomers,* scientists who study objects in space, attempted to get a closer look at Mercury's surface. But even with large modern telescopes, details

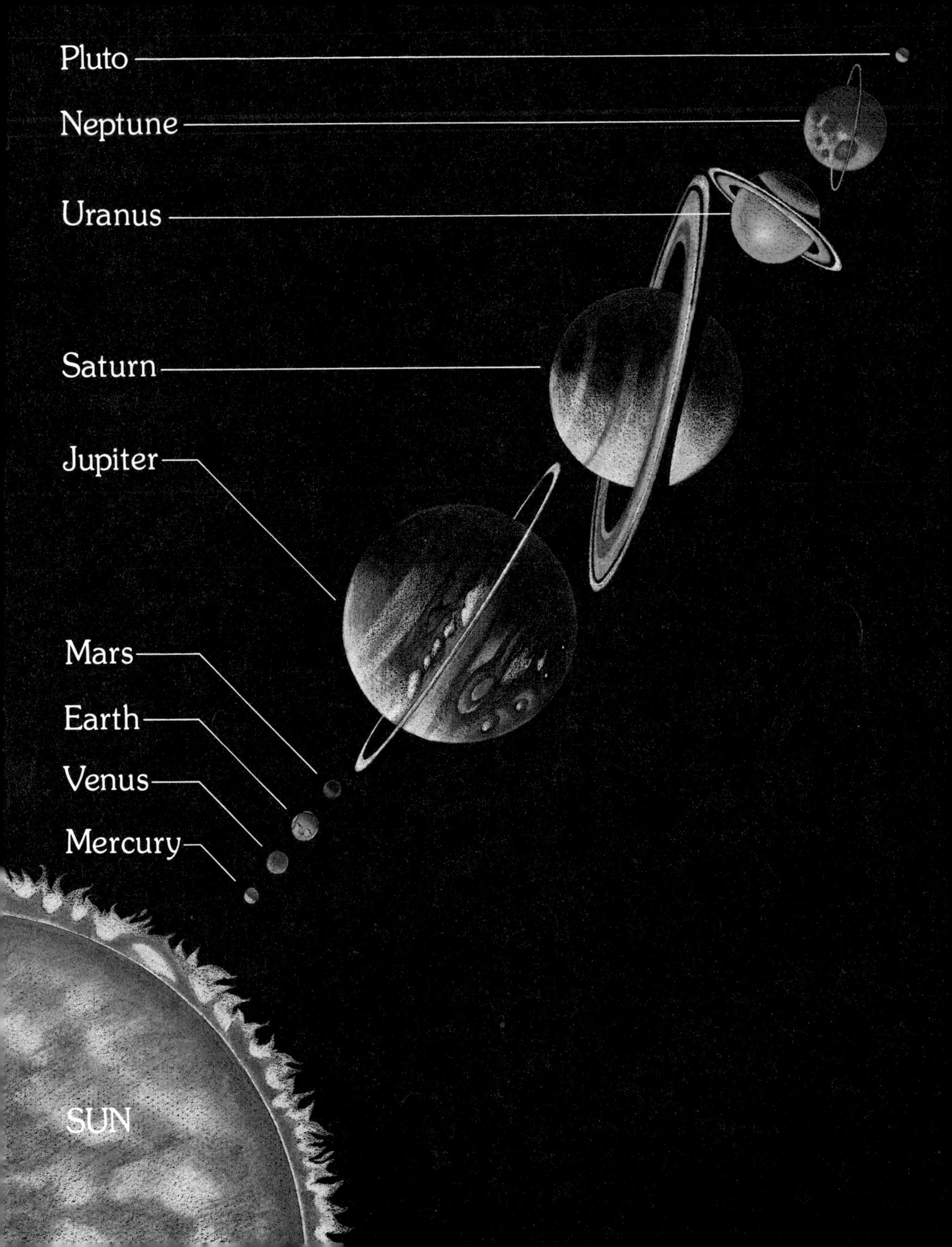

Pluto

Neptune

Uranus

Saturn

Jupiter

Mars

Earth

Venus

Mercury

SUN

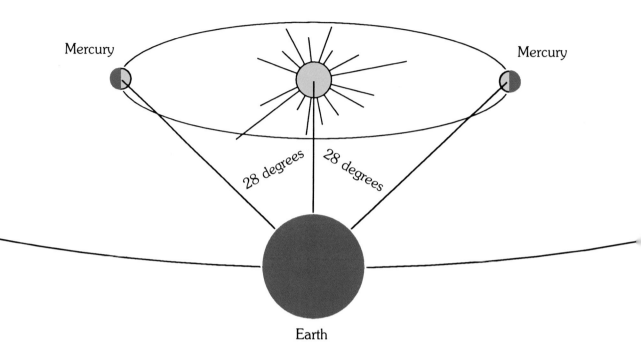

Mercury

Mercury

28 degrees 28 degrees

Earth

Viewed from Earth, Mercury is never more than 28 degrees to the side of the sun.

on its surface are hard to see. If Mercury had a mountain, for example, it would have to be at least 435 miles (700 kilometers) across just to appear as a tiny dot through the biggest telescopes. Therefore, hand-drawn maps and telescopic photographs revealed only shadowy features.

Nevertheless, astronomers formed many theories about what the planet must be like. Some astronomers believed Mercury's surface was smooth, like a billiard ball. They believed that the sun, which would have been hotter in the past, would have melted Mercury's surface rock. When the molten rock cooled, it would have formed a smooth surface. Others believed the surface was covered with *craters,* like that of our moon, or had huge mountain ranges.

Although many early ideas about Mercury proved false, other discoveries about the planet proved true. One of these discoveries was that Mercury is a very dense planet—that is, very heavy for its size. This was discovered by observing how Mercury's gravity affects objects moving past the planet. In 1841, Johann Franz Encke measured how the course of a comet passing near Mercury was changed. Mercury's gravity pulled on the comet and bent its path. The path bent so much that Encke concluded that Mercury must have a strong gravitational pull for its size.

Today, we know the reason for this strong pull. Mercury has a large *core* of iron. The core of a planet is like the yolk of a hard-boiled egg. Like the yolk, Mercury's core is shaped like a ball. Because it is made of iron, it is very dense. Above Mercury's core is a layer of lighter rock (like the egg white) and an outer surface

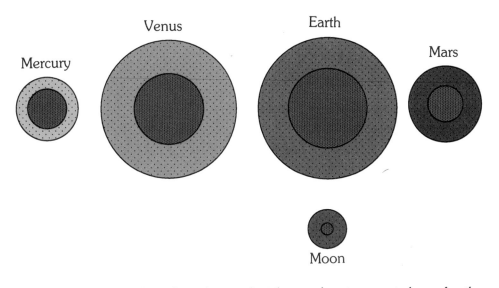

Mercury

Venus

Earth

Mars

Moon

Mercury is smaller than the other rocky planets, but its core is large for the planet's size.

called the *crust* (like the eggshell). Compared with all the other planets in our solar system, Mercury's core is huge. Earth's core makes up only about one sixth of the volume of the entire planet. Mercury's core is between one third and one half of its volume!

Because of its heavy core, Mercury has a much stronger gravitational pull than it would have if the planet

◄ Eighteen photographs of Mercury, taken by the *Mariner 10* spacecraft, were pieced together to produce this picture.

Rock and meteorite fragments are scattered across the floor of a large crater in this artist's painting of the surface of Mercury. Because of the planet's thin atmosphere, the sky always appears black.

were made of lightweight rock. Even so, the planet's small size means that its gravitational pull is not as strong as Earth's. If you weigh 100 pounds (45 kilograms) on Earth, you would weigh 38 pounds (17 kilograms) on Mercury. You would weigh the same on Mars. But Mars is more than two and a half times bigger than Mercury.

Mercury's Orbit

Mercury's orbit is in the shape of an *ellipse,* or a slightly flattened circle. Its orbit carries the planet much closer to the sun at one time during its year than at others. When Mercury is closest to the sun, it is only about 29 million miles (46 million kilometers) away. But when it is farthest, it is about 43 million miles (70 million kilometers) away. As its distance from the sun changes, so does its orbital speed. Near the close point to the sun, Mercury's speed increases to 128,000 miles (206,000 kilometers) per hour. If you could run that fast, you could circle the Earth in just 12 minutes! At its far point from the sun, Mercury's speed drops to only 87,000 (139,000 kilometers) per hour.

While Mercury is speeding around the sun, it is also spinning on its *axis,* an imaginary line running through the planet from its north pole to its south pole. It takes Mercury almost 59 days to make just one *rotation,* or spin once around its axis. That means that a Mercury year is just about as long as one and one-half Mercury days! This produces an unusual situation on Mercury. Because of Mercury's very long day and its constantly changing orbital speed and distance from the sun, the sun appears to do tricks in the sky. If you could stand at the right place on Mercury at the right time, you would see the sun rise in the sky as it does on Earth. But then, the sun would seem to change direction and go back-ward for a time before heading back to its original course. In other words, the sun would appear to do a loop in the sky. At other places on Mercury, you would see two sunrises and two sunsets!

Solar Oven and Deep Freeze

Mercury's unusual orbit has another important effect on the planet. Temperatures change wildly on its surface. When Mercury is closest to the sun, the part of its sur-face that is directly toward the sun can broil at as much as 800 degrees Fahrenheit (427 degrees Celsius). That's far hotter than your oven can get at home—hot enough

14

With the sun low in the sky, shadows stretch across the surface of Mercury in this painting.

to melt zinc. But at the poles, Mercury's temperature is low enough to permit polar ice caps. (Some recent studies of the planet indicate that Mercury may actually have thin ice caps.) And when Mercury is farthest from the sun, the part of the surface that is facing away from the sun can drop to as low as 297 degrees below zero Fahrenheit (−183 degrees Celsius). The difference between the hottest and coldest temperatures is greater on Mercury than on any other planet in the solar system.

Mercury's gravity is strong for the planet's size. But it is not strong enough for the planet to have much of an atmosphere. Atoms of gas, just like everything else, are attracted to a planet by its gravity. But when a planet is as hot as Mercury's hot regions are, gas atoms move very fast. Unless the planet has a very strong gravitational pull, the atoms will escape into space. In spite of the heat, Mercury does have an extremely thin atmosphere made of helium gas. Astronomers aren't sure where the atmosphere comes from. The helium could be escaping from the rocks at Mercury's surface, or it could be gas ejected from the sun. Regardless of how it forms, Mercury's atmosphere is only temporary. It escapes into space as fast as it is created.

Three Visits

Mercury has been visited by only one spacecraft. That spacecraft flew by Mercury three times in 1974 and 1975. The spacecraft was *Mariner 10*. It was launched by the

NASA's *Mariner 10* spacecraft had eye-like television cameras, solar panels for making electricity from sunlight, and an antenna for communicating with Earth. The two poles carried scientific instruments, and the white umbrella-like shield protected the craft from the sun's heat.

National Aeronautics and Space Administration (NASA). *Mariner 10*'s first task was to travel to Venus, the second planet out from the sun.

As it passed Venus, the spacecraft's television cameras took pictures of the dense clouds sweeping around the planet. It also measured temperatures and magnetic fields. Meanwhile, Venus's gravity bent *Mariner 10*'s path and gave a bit of a shove to send the spacecraft on to Mercury.

Mariner 10's first encounter with Mercury took place 146 days after it was launched from Earth. Reaching Mercury was a remarkable feat of accuracy. It was like tossing a baseball into the glove of a person standing 100 miles (160 kilometers) away.

After its first encounter with Mercury, *Mariner 10* sped away in a large looping orbit of the sun. Its orbit was perfectly shaped, and 176 days later, *Mariner 10* and Mercury passed by each other a second time. A third encounter took place six months later.

Details

Mariner 10 accomplished what no Earth-based telescope could. Its television camera took close-up pictures

Mariner 10's close-up pictures revealed craters of all sizes.

of Mercury's surface. Because of its closeness to the planet, objects just larger than a football field were clearly visible. This was 7,000 times better than the clearest views from Earth.

The pictures taken were just postage-stamp size and covered only small areas of Mercury. But the camera was fast, and even before the radio signal carrying the pictures reached big antennas on Earth, many more were taken. Mapmakers pieced the small pictures together like a jigsaw puzzle to produce portraits of nearly half the planet's surface.

Unfortunately, the rest of Mercury's surface was never seen by *Mariner 10*'s camera. Each time *Mariner 10* passed close to Mercury, the planet was on the same side of the sun with its same face toward the sun. The other face of Mercury was in darkness and invisible to the camera. Nevertheless, astronomers on Earth were delighted with what they saw.

Wrinkled World

To someone who doesn't know much about planets and moons, Mercury looks very much like Earth's moon. Both are bleak worlds of gray and black rock and soil. Al-

White rays extend like wheel spokes from some craters in this picture of Mercury's southern hemisphere. The picture was created from three hundred *Mariner 10* photographs. Black areas were not photographed.

though Mercury has an atmosphere, it is so thin that it is invisible. This means that the sky on Mercury, like the sky on the moon, is always black, with only the light of

the sun, planets, and other stars piercing it. Both of these worlds also have heavily cratered highland regions, smooth plains, and fine-grained soil covering their surfaces.

But there are important differences between the moon and Mercury. Instead of the mountainous terrain that makes up the highland regions of the moon, Mercury's highlands consist of gently rolling hills. Mercury also has a planet-wide system of fractures and ridges that the moon does not have. These fractures and ridges were created when the planet was still young, when the inside of the planet was hotter than it is today. As it cooled, Mercury shrank by a few miles. Like an apple that gets wrinkles when it dries out, Mercury became wrinkled with fractures and ridges.

Perhaps what stands out most about Mercury is the great number of craters on its surface. The craters were caused by the impacts of comets and asteroids more than 3.8 billion years ago. Smashing into Mercury at high speeds, these objects blasted large holes in the surface

◀ Mercury looks a lot like Earth's moon in this *Mariner 10* picture. The planet's north pole is at the top.

A low cliff, or scarp, cuts across Mercury's cratered surface in this painting. The cliff formed when Mercury's crust cracked as the planet cooled.

of the planet. After each explosion from the impacts, debris fell back to the surface to form circular mounds. The force of the explosion sometimes drove the middle point of the hole violently downward. It then rebounded to leave a central peak.

One impact that occurred on Mercury about 4 billion years ago must have been something to see. Its remains formed the Caloris basin, a series of circular ridges and cracks 800 miles (1,300 kilometers) across! The huge object that struck Mercury did so when the planet was still very young and its surface was much hotter than it is today. Waves of energy from the impact quickly traveled around the planet to the other side, where they were strong enough to break up the surface to form hills. Mercury really shook from the Caloris impact.

Lonely Wanderer

Mariner 10 finished its mission with Mercury on March 24, 1975. The spacecraft ran out of the fuel that it used to maneuver itself in flight. In its visits to Mercury and Venus it had traveled more than 1 billion miles (1.6 billion kilometers) around the sun. Today, it is still circling the sun.

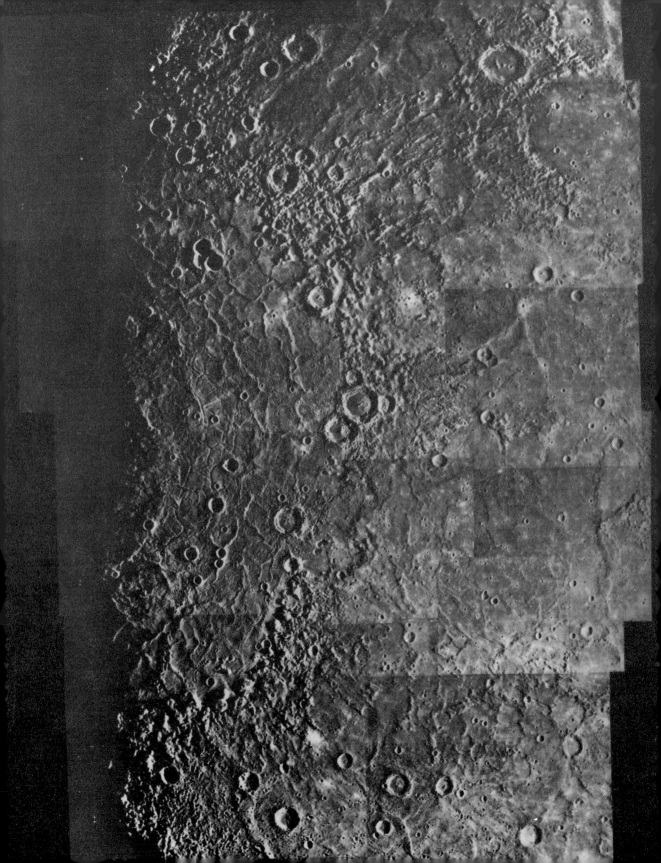

No other spacecraft has since made the voyage to Mercury. But *Mariner 10* left astronomers a legacy of pictures they still analyze today in hope of learning more about the planet closest to the sun.

◄ About half of the huge Caloris impact basin can be seen on the left side of this picture, which is made up of several *Mariner* photographs. The curved ridges were created when a huge asteroid smashed into Mercury.

MERCURY QUICK FACTS

Mercury: Named after the Roman messenger of the gods.

	Mercury	Earth
Average Distance from the Sun		
Millions of miles	36	93
Millions of kilometers	58	149.6
Revolution (one orbit around the sun)	88 days (0.24 Earth year)	365 days (1 year)
Average Orbital Speed		
Miles per second	30	18.6
Kilometers per second	48	30
Rotation (spinning once)	59 days	24 hours
Diameter at Equator		
Miles	3,031	7,926
Kilometers	4,878	12,756
Surface Gravity (compared with Earth's)	0.38	1
Mass (the amount of matter contained in Mercury, compared with Earth)	0.06	1
Atmosphere	helium (very thin)	nitrogen, oxygen
Satellites (moons)	0	1

Asteroids	Chunks of rock up to a few hundred miles across that orbit the sun.
Astronomer	A scientist who studies planets, moons, stars, and other objects in outer space.
Axis	An imaginary line running through a planet from its north pole to its south pole.
Comet	Large chunks of ice and rock that orbit the sun and stream off gas tails when heated.
Core	The dense center of a planet.
Crater	A circular or elongated hole blasted out of the surface of a planet or moon by the impact of an asteroid or comet.
Crust	The rocky surface of a planet.
Ellipse	A geometric shape that looks like a flattened or elongated circle.
Gravity	A force that causes objects to attract each other.
Inner solar system	The region of space surrounding the sun as far out as the orbit of Earth.
Mariner 10	The only spacecraft to visit Mercury.
Orbit	The path a planet takes to travel around the sun, or a moon to travel around a planet. (Also applies to the path a spacecraft follows when orbiting a planet.)
Revolution	One complete orbit of a planet around the sun, or a moon around a planet.
Rotation	The spinning of a planet or a moon around its axis.

FOR FURTHER READING

Ardley, N. *The Universe: The Inner Planets.* Englewood Cliffs, N.J.: Schoolhouse Press, Inc., 1988.

Asimov, I. *Isaac Asimov's Library of the Universe. Mercury: The Quick Planet.* Milwaukee, Wis.: Gareth Stevens Publishing, 1989.

Brewer, D. *Planet Guides: Mercury and the Sun.* New York: Marshall Cavendish, 1992.

Gallant, R. *National Geographic Picture Atlas of Our Universe.* Washington, D.C.: National Geographic Society, 1980.

Rathburn, E. *Exploring Your Solar System.* Washington, D.C.: National Geographic Society, 1989.

INDEX

ABOUT THE AUTHOR

Gregory L. Vogt works for NASA's Education Division at the Johnson Space Center in Houston, Texas. He works with astronauts in developing educational videos for schools.

Mr. Vogt previously served as executive director of the Discovery World Museum of Science, Economics, and Technology in Milwaukee, Wisconsin, and as an eighth-grade science teacher. He holds bachelor's and master's degrees in science from the University of Wisconsin at Milwaukee, as well as a doctorate in curriculum and instruction from Oklahoma State University.